FACING YOUR FEARS

FACING YOUR FEAR
OF BLOOD

BY HEATHER E. SCHWARTZ

Consultant:
Tawnya M. Ward, PsyD, LP
Clinical Psychologist
Shakopee, Minnesota

PEBBLE
a capstone imprint

Published by Pebble, an imprint of Capstone.
1710 Roe Crest Drive, North Mankato, Minnesota 56003
capstonepub.com

Library of Congress Cataloging-in-Publication Data is available on the Library of Congress website.
ISBN: 9781666355499 (hardcover)
ISBN: 9781666355550 (paperback)
ISBN: 9781666355611 (ebook PDF)

Summary: Explores the reasons why many people are afraid of blood and provides simple tips for facing this fear safely.

Editorial Credits
Editor: Donald Lemke; Designer: Sarah Bennett; Media Researcher: Julie De Adder; Production Specialist: Katy LaVigne

Image Credits
Getty Images: EyeEm/Branislav Novak, cover, Jose Luis Pelaez Inc., 9, kali9, 15, Milan Jovic, 10; Shutterstock: A3pfamily, 5, 18, Alexxndr, 21 (bottom left), Domira (background), cover and throughout, FtLaud, 6, joshya, 7, JPC-Prod, 8, Kapitosh (cloud), cover and throughout, Marish (brave girl), cover and throughout, Morakod1977, 14, November27, 13, Pixel-Shot, 19, Rattasak Pinkaew, 21 (top left), TinnaPong, 21 (right), tomeqs, 16, Viacheslav Yakobchuk, 17, Weepic, 11

Printed and bound in the USA. 4882

TABLE OF CONTENTS

Words in **bold** are in the glossary.

SEEING RED

Blood belongs inside your body. It does a lot of important jobs there. Blood helps the parts of your body work properly.

When blood is outside your body, you might feel surprised. You might feel afraid. Building skills to stay calm can help. Knowing more about blood can help too.

BLOOD AT WORK

Blood is made of different kinds of **cells**. They help your body in different ways.

Your heart pumps blood throughout your body. Red blood cells carry **oxygen**. White blood cells fight off **germs**. Other cells called **platelets** help to stop bleeding.

Blood

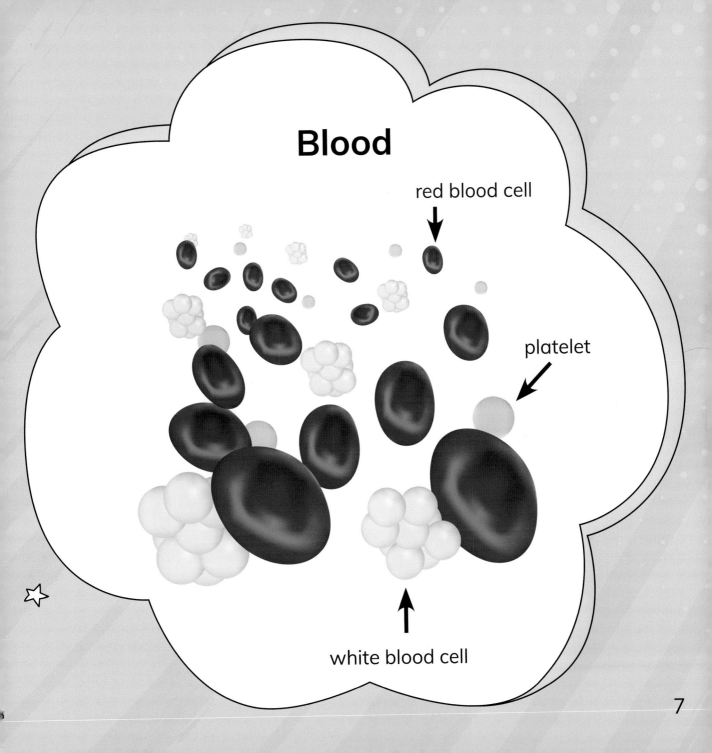

red blood cell

platelet

white blood cell

Seeing blood during a doctor's **checkup** is normal. Your doctor might **draw blood** to make sure you are healthy. You might get a shot that makes you bleed a little.

If seeing blood frightens you, try not to look. Instead, close your eyes. Then imagine something fun you like to do. You can practice this skill at home.

You might also see blood if you cut yourself. Even small cuts can be scary at times. But a small amount of blood is not cause for **alarm**.

Knowing what blood does can help you stay calm. Blood washes dirt out of a cut. It **clots** to stop the bleeding. Blood dries to form a scab that protects the cut while it heals.

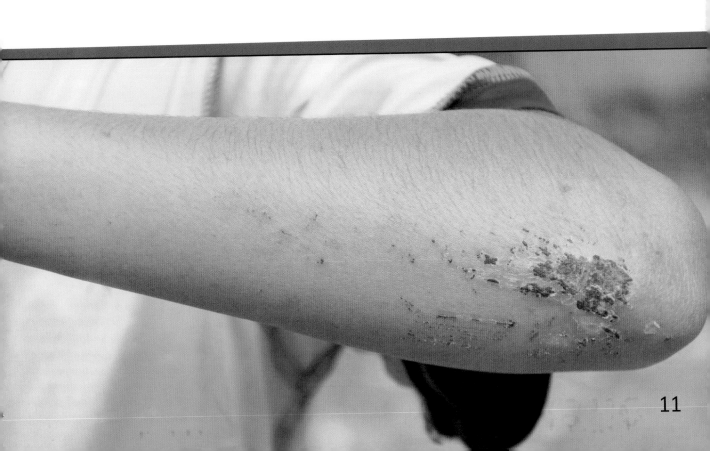

WHAT TO DO

You're riding your bike. You fall and scrape your knee. The small scrape is bleeding. You feel scared. What should you do?

Take action to feel better! First, tell an adult. They will help wash the cut and put on a bandage. The small scrape should heal soon.

You're on the playground. A friend trips and falls. He has blood on his hand. You are both afraid. What should you do?

Again, tell an adult or ask someone close by to do so. Always avoid touching anyone else's blood without special gloves on.

While you wait, keep your friend calm with a song or a story. More help is on the way!

DOCTORS AND HOSPITALS

Some **injuries** cause a large amount of blood. These injuries can be very scary. They can be serious too. But remember, doctors and hospitals are nearby to help.

If help is needed, quickly tell an adult. They might call 911. You could even make the call yourself. People at this number help with serious injuries. They know what to do next.

Blood might seem scary. But it can
be interesting too. Knowing more about
blood can help you stay calm.

Did you know human blood has a small amount of gold? Did you know snails, lobsters, and octopuses have blue blood?

Focusing on these fun facts might help you feel less fearful about blood!

CHECK YOUR PULSE

Your heart pumps blood throughout your body. It pumps more quickly when you exercise. See for yourself.

What You Need

- watch or clock
- pencil
- paper
- calculator (optional)

What You Do

1. Find your pulse point on your wrist. Count the number of beats in 15 seconds.

2. Multiply the number of beats by 4 to get your pulse rate. Write it down.

3. Do jumping jacks for one minute.

4. Follow steps 1 and 2 again.

Your pulse rate will be higher the second time you take it. Your heart is pumping faster so your muscles will have more oxygen and more energy.

GLOSSARY

alarm (uh-LARM)—a feeling of fear often caused by sudden danger

cell (SEHL)—one of the very small parts that together form all living things

checkup (CHEK-uhp)—an exam of a person made by a doctor to make sure the person is healthy

clot (KLAHT)—to become thick and partly solid

draw blood (DRAH BLUHD)—to take blood from a person's body for medical reasons

germ (JERM)—a very small living thing that causes disease

injury (IN-juhr-ee)—harm or damage to something

oxygen (OKS-uh-jehn)—a chemical that is found in the air, that has no color, taste, or smell, and that is necessary for life

platelet (PLAYT-leht)—a small blood cell that helps blood to stop flowing from a cut by becoming thick and sticky

READ MORE

Lowe, Alexander. *Adventures in the Circulatory System.* Chicago: Norwood House Press, 2021.

The Body Book. New York: DK Children, 2022.

Why Is Blood Red? New York: DK Children, 2021.

INTERNET SITES

Nemours KidsHealth: Getting a Blood Test
kidshealth.org/en/kids/video-bldtest.html

Nemours KidsHealth: What's Blood?
kidshealth.org/en/kids/blood.html

PBS Kids: Molly of Denali: Molly Learns First Aid!
wpbstv.org/molly-of-denali-molly-learns-first-aid-pbs-kids

INDEX

ABOUT THE AUTHOR

photo by Dan Doyle

Heather E. Schwartz has written hundreds of children's books. She lives in upstate New York with her husband, two kids, and two cats named Stampy and Squid. She often laughs when she feels scared, which helps her calm down.